# YOU GET TO BE YOU!

Empowering Poetry for Kids

---

Written and Illustrated by Nikki Van Ekeren

Copyright 2020 by Nikki Van Ekeren.
All rights reserved.

No part of this book may be used or reproduced in any manner whatsoever without written permission from the author, except for the use of brief quotations in a book review.

Your support of the author's rights is appreciated.

Text and illustrations copyright Nikki Van Ekeren.

Cover art and layout by Matt Van Ekeren.

Imprint: Independently published

For information regarding permission or distribution,
contact nikkivanekeren@gmail.com

To discover more about the author visit nikkivanekeren.com

ISBN: 978-1-7355066-0-9

# You are truly the only one just like you. It is an honor to be you.

Please refer to the guide at the end of the book for further discussion about each poem.

# Did You Hear The Good News?

Did you hear the
good news?

You get to be you.

You are the only one
under the sun

that's just like you
through and through.

Aren't you blessed
to have your zest?

Yay! You got the job,
you get to be you.

# Love Everyone
# The Same

As you grow older
and develop the eyes to see,
be brave enough to love
the differences in you and me.

Others may act and look
different from you,
love everyone the same
and they will love you too.

# Stretch Out

If you are feeling sad
or not too glad,

    remember to stretch out
    to feel what life's all about.

Stretching means
to open up,

    to share and
    to even show up.

        Stretch out your heart,
        it's always a good start.

        Stretch out your mind
        and think something kind.

# To Reach

I have just begun
to reach for the sun.

My heart is open wide
and I am ready to glide.

        Reaching to see the sunny side of my day
        opens up new ways to sing and play.

                Do you want to join me
                and reach?

# It Is Okay To Be Different

If you are like me
and I am like you,
then who will we turn to
when we want to be something new?

                It is okay to be
                different from the rest.
                Just remember to be you
                and always do your best.

# Trust Yourself

When you feel a message
come from your heart,
learn how to trust it
right from the start.

    You can connect to this voice,
    it is always a choice.

        Just make sure what you do
        shares kindness through and through.

You will never be led astray
when your heart guides your way.

# You Are Always Loved

Tomorrow and today,
you will always be loved.
You do not have to act or
behave in any certain way.

Know that who you are
today is always enough.
There is no need to compare
or make it more rough.

Keep on trying your best.
But know that it's okay
when the sky seems foggy
or the day is grey.

You are always loved today,
tomorrow, and forever
just as you are.

# Sharing Your Feelings

It is good to know
that you can open up
and let your feelings flow
like water from a cup.

                        It is always safe to share
                        with those around you who care.

# Sitting Under a Tree

Would you like to
sit under a tree
with me?

Let's breathe in this fresh air,
show mother nature that we care
and value all of her gifts everywhere.

The leaves of green,
the blue sky to be seen,
the sweet little dog
and even that frog.

Would you like to
sit under a tree
with me?

It feels so fun
to bask under the sun
letting our worries go
soaking up that glow.

# Let's Make A Choice

Let's make a choice
to always be our best self.

    You can use your own voice
    to express, to share,
    to love,
    and even to care.

        Let's make a choice
        to see today as a sunny day
        even when things are not
        going our way.

# Learning To Change

Have you heard
of the word cope?

It means to be able to change
and to do so with hope.

When you can
learn this way
and adjust to each day,

you can rise up and soar
in new ways than before.

## That's A Good Idea

Life is a miracle,
rest into today.
Learn how to accept
the gift of this day.

Believe that everything is
for your good,
and you will begin to thrive
as only you should.

# If I Have a Bad Dream

Sometimes at night,
when I have a bad dream
I wake up with fright
and I want to scream.

It seemed so real,
I did not like
how it made me feel.

What should I do
when I have a bad dream?

Maybe it is best
to wake up my mom or my dad.
I can ask them to help me
to not feel so sad.

When I do this, they listen.
"It was just a dream" they say.
They hug me and tuck me back in
and soon it will be the next day.

# Sometimes The Rules Need To Be Rewritten

They always say
to follow every rule
especially when
you are a student at school.

But, what if the rules
are old and stale?
What if they need a rewrite to
allow their followers to set sail?

It takes time to learn
to have the ability to discern-
which means to know
the difference between right and wrong.

If you have a gut feeling
that a rule needs rewriting,
trust yourself in the matter
even if it makes others chatter.

It may seem hard at first,
but the beginning is always the worst.
It will become easier to know
which rules to follow and which to outgrow.

# You Are Unique

Who are you?

You are totally unique
and super special.

                                      The world needs your spark
                                      or else it will seem dark.

If you feel that you need to hide,
take a breath and decide

to share your light
and allow everyone to delight.

## The Magic Is In Your Mindset

Your mindset is up to you,
even when you are feeling blue.

      Just check in with yourself
      and choose to see the light.

            This is how you create your
            mindset and begin to take flight.

# Be A Cheerleader For Joy

Jumping for joy
can feel so great,

to feel such happiness
and to appreciate.

Be a cheerleader for joy
and let others know this.

It is what makes you special
and brings everyone else bliss.

Even if another is down,
you can help change their frown.

Your joy can spread so fast
and be a feeling that will last.

# Be the Brave One

There will be a time
when you need to take a stand
and raise your hand
to show that you are brave and grand.

When you are the brave one
in your group,
you are always the leader
of the troop.

You will get to show others
that you are tough
and made up of all the good stuff.

You will get to
be the brave one
who gets things done.

Standing up for what's right
doesn't always mean
putting up a fight.

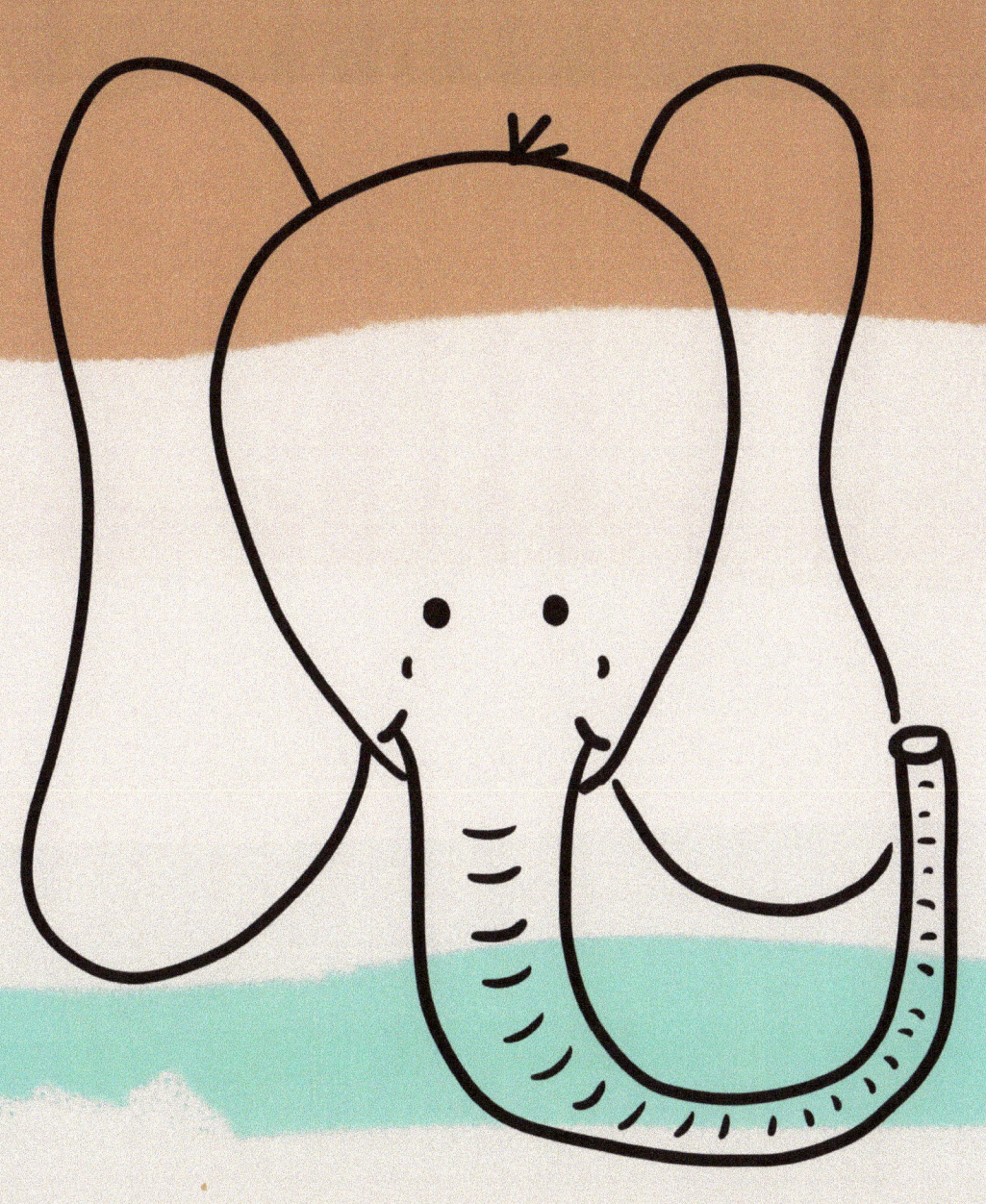

# Today, I Choose To Smile

When it is hard
to see the good today
and nothing seems to be
going your way,
it is up to you
to choose what to say.

    If you want to feel better
    and give a boost to your heart,
    you can choose to smile
    and begin with a fresh start.

As you grow and learn
that nothing is as bad as it seems,
you'll see how everything passes
and soon you will be living your dreams.

# Little Acts

Little acts
of bravery
add up
in a big way.

Smile.
Be happy.
Say "I love you."
Share something of yours
with someone else.
Stand up for someone.

It all adds up,
because bravery
is contagious.

# The Magic Of Hope

There is something magical
that comes from hope.
It is an invisible force
that always helps you cope.

    In times of great pain
    when you feel sorrow,
    hope can spark inner joy
    and excitement for tomorrow.

        Hope opens up your heart
        and allows you to embrace
        the light.
        It awakens your spirit
        while igniting your essence
        to be bright.

Hope can be shared.
Hope will never run out.
Hope will bring joy.
Hope is always the best route.

# I Need You

I need you
and you need me.
We are all connected
and it is easy to see.

You are the
only one like you
who can do
what you do.

You are needed
in every way
and others want to hear
what you have to say.

So, open your heart
and share your voice.
Listen to others as well
and always make this a choice.

# Creating The Energy Around You

Did you know
that you have the ability
to create an inner glow?

This light you infuse
has the power take
away the blues.

This bright inner spark
can take away the dark.

# To See The Sun

The sun is shining today
with no clouds in its way.

Even if the clouds were to cover its ray,
would you still be able to play?

    The sun is shining on you and me
    showering its warmth and glee.

    Yet, if it were to hide behind a tree,
    would you still be able to see?

        Maybe the idea of the shining sun
        lies inside the heart of everyone.

        Could your loving heart radiate that fun
        and share love and joy with everyone?

# Don't Hide Your Joy

You never have to hide
all of the joy you have inside.

    It is something to share
    with others with care.

        Smile from the bottom of your heart
        allowing this glow to be your art.

    You never have to hide
    all of the joy you have inside.

You will never run out
because love is what life is all about.

# Self Love

When you can learn
to love yourself all the time,

this emotion is yours
with no reason or ryhme.

# Here are some ideas for further discussion if you think that your child is ready:

### 1. "Did You Hear the Good News"

Talk to your child about positive self worth.

What makes your child excited to be exactly who they are?

You can go first and share with them something about yourself that you absolutely love.

### 2. "Love Everyone the Same"

The joy of being human is to develop the ability to celebrate one another's differences. This is an ongoing journey that we are all trying to get better at.

You can start to celebrate your own unique traits and set an example to your children.

Ask your child how they think that they are different from you.

How does your family celebrate one another's differences?

### 3. "Stretch Out"

Sometimes when we are feeling down, we tend to retreat and internalize our feelings.

Ask your child what they do when they are feeling sad?

Exercise: Stand up and spread out your arms like the branches of a tree.

How does this make you feel? Do you feel stronger? Do you feel more courage?

### 4. "To Reach"

It feels good to try to see the sunny side of life.

How does your family work to see the good in the day?

Life has its challenges. It is up to us how we perceive them.

You and your child can talk about ways in which to see the good in both the challenging and positive times.

### 5. "It Is Okay to be Different"

Our self worth can sometimes get stuck in how others perceive us. This can shape how we see others as well.

You can talk about how you embraced how you were different and how this helped you.

Ask your child if they've ever felt different and how they reacted to that feeling.

### 6. "Trust Yourself"

Developing the ability to trust yourself is a lifelong lesson.

Each day is an opportunity to flex this muscle.

You can talk to your child about the meaning of intuition and how you've listened to that inner feeling.

Ask them if they've ever heard an inner voice from their heart.

## 7. "You Are Always Loved"

Unconditional love is an honor to give and receive. Talk to your child about what this means to you.

How can your family embrace one another and not judge?

## 8. "Sharing Your Feelings"

Ask your child if they feel safe to share their inner feelings?

Encourage them to do so and ask how you can make it easier for them.

## 9. "Sitting Under a Tree"

When was the last time you and your child had a picnic or sat under a tree?

If it is nice outside, perhaps you can find a tree to sit under and read together.

## 10. "Let's Make a Choice"

Ask your child to think about a fun time in their life.

What made it fun?

How do they tell the story?

Ask them to think about a hard time in their life. What made it hard?

How can they see how this hard time actually helped them?

## 11. "Learning To Change"

Talk to your child about the ways in which you cope. How do you rise up when you are challenged?

Ask your child if they could do the same.

## 12. "That's a Good Idea"

Does your family feel like they are thriving?

If not, how can you see your life in this way?

You can also talk about gratitude. How can you look for the miracles all around you?

## 13. "If I Have a Bad Dream"

Ask your child when was the last time that they had a bad dream.

Tell them to remember that dreams only take place in the mind. They may seem real for the moment, but they are not real.

You can share with your child your thoughts on dreams. Do you think that they hold a meaning? What does your child think?

## 14. "Sometimes the Rules Need to be Rewritten"

You can discuss with your child how some adults may be trying their best, but have grown out of touch with their hearts.

You can talk about the ways in which you feel comfortable telling your children how to stand up for themselves.

### 15. "What Makes You You"

What a fun topic!

The world needs us all to show our unique light. Have fun with this topic.

Share with your child what is special about them and how your family can celebrate their uniqueness.

### 16. "The Magic is in Your Mindset"

Self accountability. Responsibility. These are personality traits that we are all continually working on.

Have a conversation with your child about what these topics mean to you.

How do you persevere when you are feeling down?

Your methods may be exactly what your child needs to hear.

### 17. "Be a Cheerleader for Joy"

Learning how to create inner joy is a learned skill. It is easy to be happy when everything is going your way, but how can you cultivate it when things are not going so well?

Ask your child this question.

Have a conversation about the last time your family tried to create joy when they were feeling blue.

### 18. "Be the Brave One"

Being the brave one or the one who speaks up can feel lonely and scary—just like with any other skill or habit, it gets easier the more we do it.

Share with your child an example of when you were the brave one.

Ask them if they have their own story.

### 19. "Today, I Choose to Smile"

It may sound cliche to an adult, but choosing to smile can truly generate an inner glow.

Ask your child how they choose to smile. What does it feel like to choose happiness rather than being sad.

Perhaps you can weave in a story about how compromising with the family is an example of this.

### 20. "Little Acts"

Every little bit helps. Every small act of courage brings inner strength, resilience and confidence.

What does your family do to help out one another?

What have you done for other families?

It doesn't have to something grand, it can be as small as picking up your neighbor's package or mail for them.

These little acts of kindness are so powerful.

### 21. "The Magic of Hope"

The magical act of hope is a topic that you can discuss with your child for years to come.

Similar to love, compassion, and kindness; hope is an invisible force that may take shape through actions and decisions.

How do you cultivate hope?

What does hope mean to you?

Share your ideas with your child. What does hope mean to them?

### 22. "I Need You"

As humans, we need one another.

Sometimes we may be the one who extends the hand to offer help, or another may extend their offer toward us.

Rather than try to fit in, take this time to rearticulate the value of embracing our unique qualities.

How does your family listen and hear from everyone in it? Ask your child if they feel heard and appreciated. How can everyone feel safe to share their voice in your home?

### 23. "Creating the Energy Around You"

Our inner spirit and energy are so powerful. Ask your child if they can sense if someone else is sad. How do they sense this? What do they do about it?

You can share with them how you use your intuition for the good and how you have tried to help others when you sense that they are sad.

### 24. "To See the Sun"

As we cultivate that inner glow, we can witness how fast it spreads. Looking at the metaphor of the shining sun as the glow within, how can we create a feeling of joy?

Ask your child how they can share this joy.

### 25. "Don't Hide Your Joy"

As your child gets older and cultivates a peer group, the tendency may be to act aloof and not as joyful as they once did.

Perhaps if you begin talking about this at a young age, they may not fall into this trap.

In what ways can you and your child share your joy today?

### 26. "Self Love"

This topic will be a lifelong journey for you and your child to infuse into your lives.

In what ways do you feel self love?

Ask your child how they feel about themself.

You can steer the conversation by sharing how you love yourself and you continue to generate this self love.

www.ingramcontent.com/pod-product-compliance
Lightning Source LLC
Chambersburg PA
CBHW042029100526
44587CB00029B/4340